Young Opinions, Great Ideas

"So that big people can see things from a little kid's eyes. Cos little kids can see what big people may not realise. Like the story of the Emperor's New Clothes, when the Emperor was walking naked and it was only a little kid that saw that the Emperor was walking naked. Little kids see things that big people may not realise and that's why I think that little kids should have a say as well".

Important quote from young person interviewed.

ontents

omment
by Andi Peters

The only way we can find out what young people think is by asking them. This may sound obvious - but it is often a forgotten option. One reason that current policy making often fails young people is that they are given little opportunity to express their concerns and priorities to decision makers.

This National Children's Bureau project demonstrates how important it is to make sure young people have a voice. Young people care and worry about their future, their friends, family, the environment and about their own and other people's health. Government proposals would benefit from the active input of children and young people.

One of the reasons I enjoy working on children's television is the enthusiastic and creative interaction with the young people involved. They are often the ones with the most imaginative and fun ideas, who are never scared about putting their opinion forward. Children's television wouldn't work if children didn't like it or didn't feel involved.

We may all have been children once but this doesn't mean we know what children think and care about today.

oreword

by Jamie Sainsbury

The Tedworth Charitable Trust is very pleased to have been able to support this National Children's Bureau initiative to gather children and young people's ideas about how NCB can develop its work in promoting children's participation in consultative processes at a national level.

The project has underlined the importance and value of encouraging young people to have their say and to make a positive contribution to their communities. It also seems clear that the research process itself has made an enormous difference to the self-esteem and confidence of those involved, and the commitment of the young researchers to this project has been a great inspiration.

My fellow trustees and I would like to thank all of them, and NCB, for having enabled us to be associated with such an innovative and successful initiative.

James Sainsbury

The Tedworth Charitable Trust

1. INTRODUCTION

A project was launched in July 1997 to find five young people to work as a team of researchers for the National Children's Bureau charity. After a painstaking sift through applications, a decision was made on who the young people should be. Because of the standard of the applications an extra two people were added to the five, making seven young, intelligent and enthusiastic people working as a team.

We first met in the December of 1997:

Emma Tolley, 15-years-old, a rising star in the world of sport and who enjoys spending time with friends.

Marchu Girma, 14-years-old and already accustomed to the National Children's Bureau, having worked with the charity on previous occasions.

Adam Stanton-Wharmby, 15 years, an ardent Newcastle United supporter and who knows every detail of every football match ever played!

Anthony Spate, 16-years-old, a music lover (but not just because of Janet Jackson's dance routines!) And also a rising comedian (but please don't ask him to tell you a joke!)

Jenny Milburn, 15-years-old, also with a great love of music and singing and will even do a little dance if you ask her nicely!

Unfortunately Robert and Emma - the other two young researchers - were unable to finish the project. Robert was denied permission to attend the meetings by the Home Office (he lives in a secure unit), and Emma, after moving into her new flat, found more exciting things to do!

The aim of the project was for us to discover what the concerns of young people are everywhere, what their worries are, and how we can make people listen to them.

We met on arranged weekends at various locations to learn research skills and techniques, and composed questions which we felt would get answers. Armed with our new techniques, skills and questions we travelled to a number of different environments such as schools, children's homes, secure units and youth centres to see what the concerns of young people are and what they want to see done about them.

We decided to interview young people with different backgrounds,different cultures and from all over the country. We did this because we wanted as wide a range of views and opinions as possible - we didn't want to leave anybody out. We think that people from minority groups are important and should never be excluded. We wanted the project to be as fair as possible so that all young people can have a voice.

We hope our research will play a vital role in telling adults what young people want and giving children and young people a voice.

Quotes

I applied to work on this project because I feel that children and young people are not listened to by adults and I want to help children. All children have the right to have a say about things that happen to them no matter what their age, religion or race.

I have always believed that young people should be heard more and I think that this is an excellent opportunity to do something about it, to be part of a big positive step.

I applied to be a young researcher because I felt that it seemed to be a good opportunity to help children and young people have a voice and be heard. It gives us a chance to voice our concerns and our worries in a sensible way.

I applied to this project because I wanted to do something that can help children and young people to have a say and be heard because I know - well every young person knows - how it feels to not be heard.

2. WHO WAS INVOLVED

We interviewed 70 young people living in Banbury, Birmingham, Bolton, Devon, Isle of Wight, Greenwich, Lichfield, Newham, Nottingham, Stockwell and Wolverhampton. The places we went to included two secure units, four comprehensive schools, one grammar school, two youth projects, one residential school and one Scout group.

We deliberately tried to get a good mix of people from different backgrounds and different age groups. Our assistant at the National Children's Bureau helped us find places to go. We also used some of our own contacts.

No. of females	%	No. of males	%
28	40	42	60

AGE RANGE

Age	Number	%
Under 11	2	3
11 years	2	3
12 years	9	13
13 years	15	21
14 years	12	17
15 years	19	27
16 years	4	6
17 years	6	9
Unknown	1	1
Total	70	100

ETHNIC ORIGIN

Ethnic origin	Number	%
Bangladeshi	1	1
Black-African	6	9
Black-Caribbean	3	4
Chinese	1	1
Mixed parentage	3	4
Pakistani	2	3
White	51	73
Other	1	1
Total	70	96

17 people (24%) said they had special needs and 33 (47%) said they followed a religion:

RELIGION

Religion	Number	%
Christian	16	23
Hindu	1	1
Muslim	3	4
Roman Catholic	3	4
No religion	47	67
Total	70	99

WHERE THEY LIVE

Where they live	Number	%
With parents	48	69
Residential school	11	16
Secure unit	11	16
Total	70	101

3. WHAT WE FOUND OUT

We asked young people some questions.
On the following pages are their answers and
our thoughts about what they said.

What concerns you most as young people?

- Drugs were a big issue, they were mentioned at a lot of the interviews with 11 to 16-year-olds. Four out of the 11 groups were very worried because there are drug users and drug dealers in their communities. The younger people (9 to 11-year-olds) were the most worried.

- Bullying was mentioned by all the groups we interviewed, especially because of colour. One group of pupils talked a lot about older pupils bullying younger ones. Young people living in the two secure units said there was hardly any bullying by other young people but one group said staff can bully by the words they use or the way they look at you. Some students from a grammar school said they get singled out because of their school.

- Most young people talked about having too big a workload at school, and a lot of pressure. There was a lot of pressure from teachers to do well, and many people complained that they didn't have enough information about courses after school so didn't know what they wanted to do next. Most people said they know that it's important to have an education to get a better job and to be a better person. I've been bullied at school.

- A lot of people were concerned about relationships; friendships were very important and one group living in a residential school thought about boyfriends and girlfriends a lot. They found it hard to have relationships at school. Many groups said that parents do listen but they don't always understand.

- Money was important, especially among older people. Only two groups said they were not really concerned about money yet, although they all said they want good jobs when they leave school.

- Many people worried about young people smoking and drinking in their area. They said they saw a lot of young people doing it in their community. A group of nine to 11-year-olds said they needed more police in community.

- Young people were concerned about pollution and the environment. They said too much litter is dumped, and that cars are bad and people should stop using them. They were also concerned about the effects on asthmatics.

Yeah, there's quite a lot of bullying [in school]

They pick on you them year 11s a lot. When you're new they pick on you, but then you get used to it

Quite a lot of people like hang around smoking, drinking, everything

They [teachers] put a lot of pressure on you to do well

[Teachers] don't really give you as much information about other courses, it's mainly go to university...I don't know what I'm gonna do next because they haven't really given me as much information as I need

I used to be bullied a lot by the older people than me, and it makes you feel very nervous...it affects your work a lot

Crime

It's a lot of teasing and a lot of pressure put on you, along with all the pressure that teachers put on you, it can really get to you. I think there are a lot of people who take drugs round here and nobody sort of realises it...I've seen a lot of people on street corners taking big sniffs out of things

There's like lots of drugs going around here nowadays

It [racism] happened to me everyday, because of my colour

Pollution around the area and rubbish just dumped

Too many bad people

Drug dealers...there's five down at the bottom of our street

We do get a good education

They should have more police coming round [to deal with violence and crime]

There should be more warning about drug dealing

We don't really get a say - we just do as we're told

You find needles all over the floor. [Our] park it's got like needles all over it

There's too much litter around everywhere... people should start using their legs instead of cars and that'll stop pollution

My mum listens to me sometimes but sometimes she says I'm talking rubbish

Education so that you can be a better person than the next one

Grow up to be someone good

Education so than you can have a better life to live

You need education to get a job and earn money

You need education to get a job when you're older. And if you don't have education you can't get a job at all

I think it's bad because if you bully people one day it will come back to you

...bullying is not a good thing to do because what goes around comes around

I think drugs are bad because you may die

I think drugs are bad for you. Once you take them you'll be addicted to them and if you're caught dealing drugs...you'll be behind bars again

Drugs take your life

There's pollution everywhere nowadays. People don't really care. We really need to clean our environment and stuff to make it a better place to live in

No one ever get's bullying in here mate [secure unit]

If I see a little kid throw their rubbish on the floor, I say 'hey' and 'put it in the bin' I think pollution's bad for people with asthma. And I think about litter sometimes. I see people eating something and throwing it on the floor and there's a bin right next to them

I think it's good to have a good relationship with friends

I live with my mum and I have two sisters and one brother. We get on well. I have a nice family and sometimes I might do something wrong with my little brother, I get the blame for it and it's still alright because my mum told me that she's telling me how to look after my little brother. But that's part of learning. Because children need to learn from their parents, so that they can know how to treat their own son

I'm living with my dad and my stepmum. Perhaps it bothers me because I ain't seen my real mum for some while back. I get pictures every now then but it's not the same

Friends are good cos when you're getting bullied they can back you up and when you need something, if they have it they will give. That's what a true friend is

Bullying is an every day thing, you can't get rid of it...staff bully us...because the staff can bully us by the way they look or just something that they say. Or intimidate, you get me? Saying something like... 'I'm going to my family at Christmas'

I will get a job, that's why I going school, to get an education which will help me get a good job when I grow up

My keyworker always tells me he'll back me up on what I say. If I'm arguing and it's right then he'll back me up on what I'm saying. But some other staff don't do that so you have to tell them and then they don't like it so they start getting mardi and saying well you're in a secure unit'...It's not like you're gonna forget that you've gone off the road in your life and you have to be brought back into the main one

Sometimes I wish I was out [of this secure unit] but it's doing me good innit in here...I've lost out on my childhood innit; being a teenager

My family's had a lot of racist attacks. When I first came from Bangladesh, we lived in Paddington, yeah? And there were a lot of whites, there was hardly any black people - only three or four in my flat. The rest were Irish and they used to take the piss. They used to like say are you Pakis and they used to cuss the black people who were our neighbours. We had black neighbours, yeah, Jamaican neighbours and they used to look out for us. Some Irish boy, he went to petrol bomb all of our flats. There was four black people in my flat and us and they went to petrol bomb our flat. He was Irish, he was only 17 and then my brothers said why are you doing this for? They were calling me Paki and everything. I just said I'm proud to be Paki, but even though I'm not from Pakistan, I'm proud to be Paki. Whatever they say, I just walk away from them, keep away from trouble

GROWN UPS complain about young people breaking in houses, yeah? But if they really wanted to, yeah, they could set up a youth group. They're not doing nothing for the youths of today. And that's why we just go on...Crime is the easy way out

All I think about most nights in [this secure unit]...is how I'm gonna change and if I'm gonna be strong enough to say no to people

Friendships just get broke when one person leaves...I could start becoming friends with them and then the next week they're gone so it's just one of those things it's just a case of ships passing at night

Yeah, or 'I'm going home at 2.15'...but I don't care, man. I don't give a damn because I know for a fact, yeah, that I'm going home in 24 weeks

And my family's at the side of me, and even my family... no matter where I am, they're there. So I don't care if they can see their's every day. I don't care

[Racism] does bother me...Just the other day I was walking down the street and I was hearing some white lady cussing other black people. That lady did bother me and I just wanted to go over there and say 'I'm sorry...you're cussing black people but you know we're all supposed to be equal and stuff'

Another racist attack we live in fear

But, sometimes, yeah, sometimes at night I do wish people were with me, man. Sometimes I wish that I shared a room, because when the light goes off at night I don't like the lock

IT depends what kind of mood they're [staff] in. If they're in a bad mood then you just don't get on with all of them. And it depends what sort of mood you're in as well

I don't even talk to staff when they're in a bad mood - forget it, man

EDUCATION is a priority, it's the key to your future

I think we all should mix together and create a better world

YOU can be bullied in all different kinds of ways, you know what I mean? Like your criminal friends man, if you know what I mean, call you, pussy

Analysis

We were not surprised by the comments about bullying, drugs and workload of school. We had not expected the comments about not being able to make relationships so much (raised by young people living in a residential school); or about some young people caring about others smoking and drinking so much. Young people can enjoy such things as drinking but this side may not have come out in the research. The young people we interviewed may have been concerned about being interpreted as irresponsible if they said so. We were surprised that the environment came up as a big issue as we know that young people think about it but we didn't realise it was so important.

So what makes these things important for young people? Young people feel under pressure about trying drugs and other things. Drugs, workload and bullying really affect young people's everyday life; they have to face these things every day.

There is a lot of worry and pressure about getting qualifications and the amount of work we have is a big pressure. Bullying affects everyone, however big you are, there is always someone bigger. Once you are bullied you might move on to do it to someone else. Young people also face pressure about having a boyfriend or girlfriend.

# Is there anything else that you think about a lot?

Other things young people worried about included:

- Teenagers thought a lot about the opposite sex and some were worried about younger kids having sex and not knowing how it could affect them.

- Sport - some people thought a lot about sport.

- Wars and nasty things - people were scared for their family being in a war, and they were scared about a war happening in England. A lot of people were worried about people abroad suffering from the result of war. Younger children were concerned about violence, crime, and people on the streets drunk.

- Many young people talked about relationships again - they said they have arguments with friends at school and are concerned about family relationships, especially people walking out. Young people whose parents have split up find it hard without both parents, and they need more money to support their family. In one of the secure units young people said staff wind them up and take it out on them when they're moody.

- Pressure - many people said they don't want to go to school because there's too much work which means too much pressure. Other pressures include: pressure to get money, so people do it illegally; and being pressurised by friends to do things you don't want to.

- Quite a lot of young people were scared about dying - in car, plane and boat crashes - so they don't like travelling. They were also scared about their parents dying. Lots worry about heaven and hell and some were scared of dying in pain.

I think about violence .... dying

"Quotes"

'I hope I don't have an argument tomorrow in school' or something, and.... like that

Mostly, I think about how I don't wanna go to school, especially all the work you're gonna get, the homework and the course work. And they give you too much pressure

Yeah, I worry a lot about what's gonna happen when I leave school, or about getting a job

It's sort of like very hard with my mum because she's got this bad kidney disease and my dad's left and he doesn't support us in any way and...we don't have any washing machines or anything like that, so we have to do all the washing by hand. We don't have that much really

My mum and dad got divorced before I was born well, just before I was born, and then my sister walks out on me and my mum about six months ago but she's moved back now because mum's been drinking - she's becoming an alcoholic

Dad - he like gets depressed all the time...he just gets depressed all the time and he doesn't speak to us for days and then he just like stamps out of it, and you just never know what mood he's gonna be in when I get home...so it's a bit of a lottery when you go home

I'm worried about, when I go on a plane with all crashes and everything that's being going on...I'm gonna crash, and then I'm going to die. I'm scared of dying

I've got a baby, so money's difficult I get really, really scared sometimes...

because... two of my uncles, they were both in the Gulf War and they said it was horrible out there because people were having their skin taken off their backs by these bombs, and every time I hear there's a crisis in Iraq, I'm always getting really scared because they'll come and bomb us...It really, really scares me

...there's lots of things that get a young person like me scared...cos all the horrible wars that's going to be happening that gets me worried - Iraq and the America thing, that gets me worried cos I don't really want to see a war right now and all the things that's been happening in the world and all the suffering and all the pain that people's been going through in Africa, in Asia and all the countries.... it needs to stop. People need to look into themselves and say 'this is what I need to do to stop these people suffering'

What I think about a lot is when my parents are going to die and I don't like thinking about that. I think about what's going to happen to me when I'm older. And I don't like going into planes, cos when I'm in a plane I think it's going to crash, it's going to have a crash landing

I'm scared to die, cos when I was six my mother told me everyone has to die. From then on I'm scared to die...Cos sometime, I think, if I die, there's going to be a day, a judgement, when God's going to judge you, so that you're going to go to heaven or hell

You get pressured into things by your friends

The problem about sex, yeah, young kids under the age have that and then, do they realise what it could do to them?

"Q"

Too many pubs, they come home drunk and fighting

You have the groups of friends who sort of go round in gangs now and they don't actually mix in with any other groups in our class. We've got about five groups of people and they never talk to each other they just talk in their own groups

Staff **winding up young people**

Too much fighting, too much violence

Analysis

We expected to hear young people talk about the opposite sex as hormones are 'kicking in with a vengeance, they wear toe-capped boots'. One day someone from the opposite sex likes you and another day they don't ; one day a friend is a friend and another day they fancy you and you just want to be a friend. One researcher thought it would come up because it is important to have relationships with family and friends. Everyone knows someone who has divorced parents and the fear about loss of a parent or being on your own, worry about Dads getting depressed, parents who won't talk to you for days, parents in moods and you can't talk to them when you need to and you have to bottle it all up. This is much more of a worry to young people than we expected.

We were surprised to hear how much they were worried about war. Adults don't talk to young people about dying and so they worry about it more. They see their grandparents die and they think about what will happen when they are older but they do not get talked to about it. It builds up. Death is in the news a lot but overall it is just not talked about enough with young people. Interestingly the groups that talked about death were mostly led by the black young people. The groups that talked about racism were mostly led by the black young researchers and those who talked about residential school said more about it to the researcher who had that experience. Black young people live in environments that more often seem to have only one Mum or Dad and live in places where they see violence and death more often as part of daily life, it depresses them and they think more about it.

Thinking about war can be driven by experience for example, if you have relatives who have experienced war. The fact of a current risk of war when the interviews were being done had clearly got young people thinking. They were taking interest in and had views on the news of war in the papers and on TV.

Do you think adults understand what really matters to you?

The majority of people felt that adults do not understand, particularly:

- parents, with regards to not listening, understanding and making rules;

- teachers - young people felt that teachers did not understand or listen to the opinions and views of young people, and that teachers were unaware of the problems faced by pupils.

- There were strong feelings on MPs. Some young people who were questioned felt that MPs were only working for the rich, while others felt that MPs work too hard on the problems that don't really affect the 'real' people. In another interview, all of the young people agreed that MPs and councillors showed fake interest in the opinions and ideas of young people, and labelled young people as a risk to the community.

- The majority of the younger interviewees felt that GPs were rude to them and treated them differently to an adult. Older young people felt that they would rather visit their GP than a health clinic or anywhere else, while in another interview young people thought that generally doctors were nice and approachable, but could still do better.

- The general feeling was that social workers were OK. In one interview, it was stated that social workers understand them best as they work with children all the time, on a one to one basis. They felt that social workers can recognise problems and have a better understanding of a variety of problems.

Our social worker listens to our problems and helps us

"Quotes"

[Parents] may not be bothered or interested

I just think it's difficult to have a say with your parents because they sort of say 'Well, it's my house' you know, 'You're gonna abide by my rules and you're not gonna really have a say'

I think Members of Parliament and local councillors just like doing things for adults

I wouldn't say that they [parents] really understand me cos they're on a different level to me. They were once young, I know, but things were different from way back then and way back now. They don't understand the situations that we have right now

Some people, their parents understand them and they don't understand them...most people when they're in trouble, they don't tell their parents

Yeah, they [GPs] do understand. Sometimes they do and sometimes they don't, because there are certain things they haven't found a cure for like cancer and AIDS and other things, but they're working on it

No they [MPs] don't. They're in the rich life, they're in the fast lane. They always talk about rich people. They do try to help us in some way, but they don't really, like, what's his name, Tony Blair?

You go up to ask them [teachers], to ask to put the blind down because you can't see the board or something, they just go and tell you to sit down and you can't do the work

Some doctors treat you like adults and others treat you like kids

You ask 'can I have a calculator' and he says 'You don't need one there's an abacus'!

They [MPs] do understand some of it, but not all of it. Because they've never seen how little kids live...and they've never seen how the poor people live...I'm not saying that Tony Blair should [be] absolutely poor or something like that but he should understand what we're going through

Teachers - they understand a few things but they don't understand the situation that we've been going through as little kids

He [Education Minister] doesn't know that we've got a social life in our spare time

The only person that understands me is my sister, because if I tell my dad they're gonna say 'It's your fault, you're the one who's doing this'

My grandparents have really old fashioned ways

Some younger teachers know more about life today

I wouldn't say anything personal [to my doctor] because he's dad's friend

[Teachers] are too fond of themselves

They suspended me [from school] for wearing an earring at the top of my ear

But I think teachers have a sort of better outlook than parents

They'd [parents] like to help but they just don't understand

They [teachers] don't get to know you enough because there are so many of you

They're [MPs] sitting behind fat desks and earning loads of money

All they [councillors] do is they come round here [secure unit] every so often, take a look, shake everyone's hands and piss off again

No, they [councillors] must be doing research and other stuff like that

They [social workers] see you as like more dangerous that you are, man, sometimes

My grandmother used to understand me but now she's dead. Nobody understands me really

We went to meet him [MP] at the Houses of Parliament and he showed us round and we went to 10 Downing Street. And he asked us things, what bothered us and all that. We told him and he said if we need any help, just ask him

A friend has had a social worker. She used to take him out everywhere, cos his parents like didn't give a damn about him

Your parents do, but not the staff

They don't put anything what's good about you [in secure unit reports], they just try and put all the bad things about you

It's weird how kids talk about teachers as if they're a different species

They [parents] think they can care about you enough but they don't actually know what your deepest problems are because they won't ask most of the time

They [youth workers] only, most of them are normally like nice and like kind to you, but it's just, it's just not enough, you know, really, not enough nice people around that really, really wanna help you, just a couple of them. Everyone else just thinks you're a kid

Like this recent argument about homework. I reckon that we should have a say in how much homework we do

They should interview some kids and ask them their opinion and then decide. You know, just randomly take people, you know from each group

Because it's like being told what to do behind your back, basically

It'll be like adults running the world all the time, really. And us being like guinea pigs

Like when I first come here we didn't have a football pitch, or a tennis court up there, but the student council, when that were come in, they got us a new tennis court and a new football pitch and even goals up there now

[about MPs] they're old farts, to me. They don't give a damn about children. Like just the other week, the Education Minister has announced two and a half hours worth of homework for 15- to 16-years-olds

They [teachers] don't understand. Every time someone is telling the truth, they always get it twisted, they get it wrong

Analysis

We were not surprised that young people feel adults do not understand them. Relationships with adults are not as strong as they should be - they should work as a team more. Communication is not what it should be - it's the 'I'm big you're small, I'm right you are wrong' kind of attitude (from Matilda film).

Loads said their parents did not understand them-this was a surprise, it came from the teenagers. We all turn into 'Kevins' (one of Harry Enfield's characters) as far as they are concerned. Parents find it hard to adapt to young people having a mind of their own. They think about young people as their little babies. They only care about school and studying and think 'once you are out of my hair, good'.

Parents should realise they have to earn our respect, and they should just respect us for being their children: we should not have to do more.

Some parents are OK, some are bad and some are good - it depends on the background your parents have had. It can be that your grandparents were really strict but your parents are OK. Young people will end up quite a bit like their parents which could be good or bad or may be scary. The fact that you may follow the same pattern again and again is both boring and scary, especially if the pattern is a bad one.

While teachers are there to teach they have to have other things to talk about. Teachers think they have authority and can just say 'shut up'. Teachers need to understand they are preparing you for the world not just teaching you a subject. They need to be more sociable and to understand more about young people's experience for example, bullying. Young people need more time with your tutor group to have open discussions.

We are not at all surprised about the views on MPs. Young people have low expectations of MPs. We think MPs don't do anything, so that fits. It is hard to relate to MPs. Black young people felt that councillors and MPs should live in their area so they can better understand it. Tony Blair should go and live there. The only group that were positive about their MPs were the ones who had met him and he had answered letters and taken some to the House of Commons. It helps if MPs and royals get out there and meet young people.

GPs and other health people: the views were mixed. Some said GPs understand them but it was interesting that out of all adults, the positive comments were about the health people. It did not match with our own experience so it was a surprise how well thought of GPs are. We were surprised to find out they have the time to talk to young people when they are so busy.

Social workers should be the best at understanding young people given that they are trained to work with young people, so they should be a lot better than other adults. Those we interviewed said that social workers can be OK but some were not and they should all be. Social workers should be much better than OK but they are not.

We're trying to help children and young people to be heard more. Do you think children and young people want to have a say?

EVERYONE wants a say especially in:

- **Building clubs and leisure centres - buildings that they will use.**
Young people think there should be more going on for them especially after school because there isn't a lot. They want to have a say in the building of sports facilities and youth clubs because, after all, it's for them.

- **Fostered and adopted children should have a say as to their home placement.**
Young people said they should have a say about where they're going to live. They feel that they don't have a say and the people just put them in a placement. They should have a say because it affects them.

- **Family decisions including where they live.**
Young people said they should have a say in this - it shouldn't just be the parents. Everyone's point of view should be taken in account. Some young people said that their parents say they can't have a say because it's their house. The young people think that's wrong. They think parents should take into account what's important in their lives as well. They want a say in their family life but they don't always get opportunity.

Young people said they are not treated as living people, even though they know what's going on in their lives.

- **Health decisions - healthy eating and choosing their own doctor.**
Girls found it hard to talk to male doctors. Some girls said they thought it was terrible that parents wouldn't let them change

- **Education - young people want to choose their own lessons and school.**
Most young people said it would be more fair if you had a choice in lessons because it's you who's having to do the subject.

- **Government decisions affecting them.**
Young people said they wanted to help make government decisions. They said that the Government don't treat us as important. One group of younger people said the Queen should help more. Another group said that professionals think they know everything but don't. Most young people said that they should have a say in new laws and government decisions if they affect us. But they also said we have to understand the laws first.

"Quotes"

There **should be more going on for us, like things to do after school. There's not a lot of stuff**

Sometimes **your parents say to you, 'Oh it's none of your business. You don't have to worry about it and everything'. It's like I wanna know about things like that**

I **think that the children should have a say in the rules and it shouldn't just be the parents' point of view of what you should and shouldn't do. I think that children should put down some rules for them as well**

It's **our life. They should have a say like the Queen says everything, Tony Blair says everything. He makes the rules, why should we not make more rules?**

Just **because they're [the Queen and Tony Blair] important and we're not, they don't really treat us as important, so we're not able to say much**

I **don't see the Queen doing anything about it [homelessness]. She's got more money than all of us**

About **the things that they see as important in their lives and what they think should improve in the world**

I **got a man, a male doctor, and like if I got a girly problem I can't exactly go up to him, because it's gonna be embarrassing**

I **would change to a female doctor, but my parents won't allow me to**

It's **like their [parents] house and you have to do what they say, as long as you're in their house**

Because **like sometimes you really want to be heard, and like you don't know when that time will happen, and like as we're here tonight we're telling you what we want to happen, so I think it does help**

They **think, the professionals, they know everything about us, but they don't. We know what's going on inside our heads, and we're living people so why don't they just leave us alone?**

People **in foster and residential care should have a say about where they're gonna live and stuff**

We **should have a say in new laws and government decisions if it affects us**

Most kids would like to have a say in their family life

Don't have no say [in foster and residential care] - they just put you in a place

Yeah, I reckon you should have a choice [about lessons]. Think it's fair, if you had a choice

And everyone's supposed to like be saying, yeah, that's what we wanted, but when you're down there, then you've got kids like playing football, like painting goals on the back of the building and that, and then you get in trouble for it. Like why didn't they ask in the first and just build a football pitch and that saves all the vandalism, doesn't it?

We got youth centres around where I am and er, like, you get - they build a building, they say yeah, it's great and everything and all you've got is a pool table

I mean like, what's the new law that's come out - has it come out yet, or not? About that if you're under 16, you have to be in by 9 o'clock or something? You're going to be getting kids...hundreds and hundreds of kids getting picked up every night for that

They're going to be hiring HGVs and putting blue lights on them [to deal with curfews]!

There are a lot of children who would have valid things to say [to the Government]

Analysis

Yes, everyone wanted to have a say - this was not a surprise and it is the same as our own experience. We are not surprised that young people want more choice within their education. A few young people felt that there was no point in having a say in Government decisions that they do not understand. But we want to learn - we know our limits and where we need help.

Young people should be able to choose their school and not have it imposed by the views of the last school you went to. You might be better staying at a school you are doing very well at than be pushed to go to a tougher school where you will be under pressure and maybe not do so well. Some schools keep people out because of the young person maybe not getting all As. They should take children with potential they can build up and not just the ones that are already known to be an A student. If they are seen to help students get better, to become A students that would be better for the school image and the morale of teachers.

We were surprised that young people talked about the Queen. The views about the Queen were from young people who were all white, younger and lived in poor areas. They saw her as too rich - with everything. They see themselves as the same as her but money is a big divide. It is hard to relate to Royals.

Why is it so important that children and young people have a say?

The results from this question are about adults and children.

- The majority of people felt that it should not just be adults having a say in things. Children should have a say in things as well because adults are not always right.

- Children and young people feel they are being locked out of what is happening around them. They want to make decisions that affect them. One of the groups felt very strongly about the need to set up a children's government. They thought that the government should ask young people about things, for example homework, before they make laws about it. They also said that there should be a national figure to stand up for children's rights - someone famous like a pop or sports personality. Young people felt that it's important to get their views across so adults can know what children and young people are thinking.

Quotes

Because if you don't, other people won't have a chance. Something might happen and we wouldn't have got a chance to say anything. Nobody would be there to do anything

Because like, because they have to hear us out as well. It's not everything that the adult is good at. Some children are more brave minded than some adults

If they interview or ask some children, teenagers, what kind of youth club they'll be interested in then I think it would work much better. But if the adults just got together and say, 'Right we're gonna do a youth club' well then it just wouldn't work

Most of the decisions that grown ups make like in the council and stuff affect the children

They [adults] think they know what we want, but they don't necessarily

They [adults] just assume that we still want the same things as we've always wanted, like swings and slides somewhere

We're gonna grow up and be like the next adults

So that big people can see things from a little kid's eyes. Cos little kids can see what big people may not realise. Like the story of the Emperor's New Clothes, when the Emperor was walking naked and it was only a little kid that saw that the Emperor was walking naked. Little kids see things that big people may not realise and that's why I think that little kids should have a say as well

Little kids, they know stuff...they know what is not good and they saw old people, big people doing those things and they look and they say 'that's not good'

A lot of money's spent on like all this being done up [school] when it could've been spent on a lot more things to help us

The government launched this thing about taxes...and they thought about all these adults who would sort of get better in their jobs or something like that, but they didn't actually think how the children would be affected at all I don't think, because all these fuel prices going up has made like it's harder to keep my horse and it's getting quite a struggle to keep it, you know

Because we're the future

Everyone can voice their own opinions and make themselves heard

It's important for young people to say, cos they're expressing their feelings

It affects us and all. It don't affect adults. It affects kids more than it does adults

If kids can get across what they need and what they want they've got more chance of having a happier life, not getting into crime and that

Because we're human

Cos we know more than adults

No, we know what we want

Because when you go on about people saying what should we have for children in the future? We know, and...adults they don't know what's good for children. We know what we want - it's like schools, we get too much homework!

Oh yeah, we get too much homework. Like we get three pieces of work and we've got to spend an hour on each one - that's three hours. It's not fair

Because we're human...I think everybody, no matter who you are and what you are, should have a say, have an opinion, should be listened to, no matter what

...because you need your say because if you got someone to like ask, or you need something, you need to say

I think, yeah, you should have a say. If someone says something to you, you gotta tell them what you feel as well, if you know what I mean

Because they're [children] just as important as adults

Analysis

There is not much for us to say here because we expected to hear all this! We think that having young people's views as well as adults would help the world be a better place.

Which groups of children and young people do you think get missed out when it comes to having a say?

Most young people said that teenagers are missed out when it comes to having a say: the reason being 'because they are half way from being an adult and a child'. Some young people felt very strongly about teenagers being left out.

Other people said to be missed out are:

- Younger children - many young people said that some young children have more ideas than older ones.

- Disabled children and young people were also mentioned in three interviews.

- Young people with problems such as drugs, was also mentioned.

- One group said that people 'in the middle' get left out - the people who are not really rich but don't have problems. They felt strongly that people in the middle like themselves should be listened to and involved more.

- Ethnicity was also mentioned by 10 to 13-year-olds; they felt that all people should be treated equally and not discriminated against.

We're not all muggers

Some little ones have got more ideas than the teenagers. They like, they get left out

People who've got problems

People who like take drugs and things like that, they're just totally out of the picture

It's all kinds of people, innit?

I reckon that teenagers get missed out a lot

Kids who can't actually get there to do it, like. Kids in secure homes, you know

You don't get to vote do you [if you're locked up]. Even though you're locked away you should still get a say in how your country is going

..handicapped or disabled

They should have more facilities for disabled people...even in the youth club they've got toilets [which] are blocked by crates, so that you can't use the disabled toilets. We can't get in them

People like us, innit [in secure units]?

It's mostly - the short people. We have lots of short people in our class and they don't really get seen. 'They don't have a say. They are sitting down and the teacher tells them to 'stand' and they go 'no really stand up' and they're really standing up and they think that they're sitting down. There's lots of people who are short and people need to see them and ask them questions as well

Sometimes though it's people that are just like...people at home...that just live at home with their mum and dad, they've got problems too, as well. I think they should have their say as well...because...everybody thinks, yeah, well, they're just, nothing's wrong, but sometimes it is, so, I think they should be given a say as well

That's how you need to get things out in cases like these, man. Because look at them instances where kids have been raped and they [social services] don't know

Analysis

No surprises, those they listed are all minority groups and so do not recognise they have as strong a voice as they have. We were glad they said they should be listened to. There is a tendency to stereotype for example, teenagers as moody and aggressive, mad, with minds of their own, likely to go on the wrong path, parents tip toe around always thinking they will do something bad like just leave home, take drugs or have a bad mouth. So parents are scared of talking to their young people in case they get on the young person's nerves. Adults move aside from teenagers, they are frightened of teenagers. Adults can dictate to children and they cannot to teenagers. The papers add to the stereotype for example young people as muggers. We are sometimes seen as big children and giant children are scary. Adults think of teenagers as children's minds in adult bodies, a dangerous combination.

How can we get these children and young people more involved so they do have a say?

Young people had some really good ideas about how people who are missed out can have a say:

- Adults should involve them more in making decisions; many young people think there should be a separate voting system for children.

- Adults should let them know their views are important and wanted.

- Build links between young people and adults to say what young people want.

- Do more interviewing like we have done; get the TV to film these type of interviews.

- Have child juries when children commit crimes; experiment with young people in adult situations.

- More advertising; send letters, leaflets, inform us on what's going on, come and look at what's being done.

- Have a famous person to stand up for children; have a person that just deals with young people and their concerns, that can pass the information onto other adults, so there's a fair point of view from everyone no matter who you are.

We need to feel we are being heard

It should've been kids who decided. Guilty or not guilty. It shouldn't have been adults

Getting more involved in like making decisions

I think they should have a separate voting system...so you've got like...a kid's one and an adult's one

Inform us and tell us what's going on

Get ads in the train. Get the BBC to come down and film us or something

Come and have a look. Start by putting the homeless people in a home

Stand up and tell them that they can get involved

And that we should give them [homeless people] a meal - a hot meal like soup or something like that

And you should have like place for people who's hooked on drugs where they can go there and they can stop

Have like a person that just deals with children, children's cares and things like that, an adult who just listens to children, what they want to do. Yeah, just total fair point of view of everybody, doesn't matter where you're brought up or what you're like or where you're from

You can maybe have a few adults involved, like an organisation where adults are involved but it's children who are the main people. And then at least if the children won't be listened to, the adults will pass over their opinions and maybe then they'll be listened to

Make them feel important

Yeah, like their view is like wanted

I reckon they should experiment, you know, young people being a jury in the courtroom. You know like, it shouldn't be [just adults] like when the James Bulger murder happened in '92

Analysis

We were surprised to think young people would want to be on a jury. It would depend on the contribution young people would have in the final decision. We think they should be able to express their views but not be responsible for the decision.

To get celebrities advocating for children is a really good idea. NCB could make this a reality. They need to get celebrities who are known to young people not just to other adults. Young people need to think that it is a cool thing to do to be involved in these sort of things. Having a celebrity attached would make it seem cool to young people.

How can adults run children's charities so that children and young people can be heard?

We gave some examples for the young people to think about:

- taking part in a charity's annual reception
- helping with research and project work
- helping to manage projects
- speaking to professionals at conferences and meetings
- taking part in the Board of Management meetings
- helping choose staff for jobs

- taking part in competitions
- helping to prepare materials for adults and children
- being part of a group which helps charity staff run projects and research
- taking part in meetings with other young people at the charity
- helping to run conferences where adults have to listen to young people.

The main points which were raised by the interviews were:

- The majority of young people interviewed felt strongly that attending NCB meetings and annual receptions was a good idea.

- A suggestion by one group of young people was to have a local presence accessible and interesting to children and young people.

- Young people would rather speak to young people because in several interviews, the majority of young people agreed that adults don't listen all the time, and they don't really understand young people. A point raised in one interview was that although working at the NCB was a good idea, young people felt that they would still not be listened to, and that the work would not be taken as seriously as adults are.

- Some of the young people in another interview felt that, although they would prefer speaking to other young people, they also think that speaking to influential professionals is good, because it is a more direct way of putting their views across.

- Young people also felt that they should be involved in the production of leaflets to avoid the boring ones made by adults. If they had an input, and used their own ideas and imagination, they feel it would have more appeal among young people.

- A suggestion from one interview was to have more school councils, because lots can get done through them.

- One group suggested having a students council in the Government. They said that care would have to be taken about who is chosen so that people from different backgrounds are involved, and only those who take it seriously.

- Other thoughts which were stated in one interview were how some young people felt wary of asking an adult for help due to the peer pressure and bullying which could arise.

- Some young people were not very hopeful about adults listening to them, and others thought that adults were out of touch with them. Many young people said that young people carrying out research is a really good thing.

- The young people also said putting adverts about the charity in magazines and newspapers would help. The charity could offer training for young people, for example on interviewing.

"Quotes"

There should be kids, like on a council or something. You know where you have a council for kids. I think there should be one, so they can say what they think

Well, people are getting into trouble after school like with smoking and stuff - hanging around, because they haven't got anything to do. So it's the council who should take care of stuff. Help us to be able to do stuff after school so we don't get into trouble

I'd rather speak to you lot [young researchers]. You're better

I can't talk to social workers. I find that they always try to tell you what to do

I think we should be able to vote

I think what adults don't realise is that they were children once and they were treated just as badly, even worse sometimes

I think [it would be] better if we tell you like what to do and then like the adults go and put it forward to people...because...if it was like a registered thing and you'd done a big survey they'd like go 'Oh maybe they have got a point there then'. They'd listen to you more than they would to us

They don't realise that it's like the 90s and everything's changed

It's a good idea for children to help run conferences, where adults have to listen to and learn from young people, it's like the children would be the adults!

Helping to run conferences - that'd be fantastic, I reckon!

We'd be in charge [when running conferences], sort of for once, and like... they'd have to respond to our views, instead of us responding to their's most of the time

When we... have our assemblies to do what we feel on the fourth of the week, if the charity did one that would be good. There's a lot of things that we can be heard on - if we have assemblies every now and then and then the adults have assemblies. The adults [could] sit down and the kids... come to them and say whatever. I don't think they will actually do it, knowing the staff in the school, but it would get a word through

We have a leaflet sent home every month about what's going on in school, what's going to happen and they [could] put in a page and tell them what the kids want to say and what they think...Just send it home to the parents

Listen to us

Asking like everybody [with regards to research and project work], not just certain parts of the country, just go round asking everyone and then, like you can't just do everybody's needs, so you have to find like an average or a medium and that'll tell you what most kids want

They're [leaflets] just black and white and boring. If children, or a teenager, had a say in how to write it then it would be much more interesting and would appeal to teenagers more I think

Well, if you've got a youth justice worker like mine now, you ask him to do something. You ask him - can you come up for my next review? No he's too busy to come up for your review...it's like once in a blue moon he comes up to my review

They [adults] would say something like 'Yeah. Yeah, that's a good idea' and then move on to the next one or wouldn't take it into consideration. And they would like be surprised that we've got our own ideas, when we say we want this, they go, 'No you don't, you want this' and they go and like just tell us what we want

You know when they do this, where they take adults to primary schools, who's in prison and that, then they turn around and tell you what it's like in prison. These kids they don't realise, because they think well it's going to be years before I can go to a prison, but they don't realise there's secure units. And I reckon if they were to get kids from places like this to actually go to the schools and they'll see how young - I mean we've got 12 and 11-year-olds on our unit. Take them to the primary schools, they'll realise how young you can be when [you're locked up]

I hate social workers, I hate youth justice workers...cos they make me sick really

[About choosing teachers - in a secure unit]...you can choose people that know things and have been there and done things...and can understand. If you go to the teacher of a normal school and told her to work here, she wouldn't have a clue, she just wouldn't have a clue

[About children running conferences] That's sometimes the only way kids can get it across, because like no-one else listens otherwise, unless they like sit in that chair, handcuff themselves to the thing like!

At the end of the day some people do it [cut themselves deliberately] for attention and that, but most people just carry on winding you up and that and then at the end of the day you've just got no choice and like if you've done it once, you feel yeah, that helps. But it only helps for a short period but then when you stop and look at your arms and stuff like that, you think why am I doing this?

[Let] kids vote and adults vote

Yeah, we should vote for our prime minister

Tony Blair, all he's done is change the rules, like, you have to be in at 9 o'clock, change rules, like more homework and it's like not fair on us, cos we're only kids and we've got to have a bit of fun in our life

Adults, like, when we want some new clothes, they just buy us an appalling top, like a brown top, cos they used to wear them. We've got different fashion now

Do things like this [young people carrying out research], innit?

I think it's better coming from a young person, because like, you know what I'm saying, like, you're on the same level

Put [questionnaires and leaflets] in shops and superstores because people like go into them

[About the benefits of direct contact] Well it looks like you're making an effort if you actually gave them to people. It'd look like you're making more of an effort than just a postcard

Yes! [we want to be involved] so people can be more aware about what bothers us

Analysis

Young people's experience of asking for help is not good, for example spelling. Young people are not used to being listened to, they do not value their own views and experience as a consequence. Young people can help adults get things done faster because young people's views can help direct them. There is a fear among young people that if they ask adults for help they would have the mickey taken out of them by other young people.

It's a good idea to have small scale charity representation across the country. They are too isolated at the moment. If it there was a local site for young people to reach out to that would be good. The charity needs to have a way of young people sharing their views and working with the charity in each area. This should be a place where physical meetings can take place too.

They spoke to us because we are their own age and they knew we would not judge them. There is a problem in that it is adults that can take action so just talking to young people may be easier but it may not be sufficient.

Young people were more relaxed about having a discussion over issues with young researchers and to getting a real debate going rather than trying to impress or just say yes or no as they would to adults. They may try and please adults but that is not an issue with young researchers.

What else can we do to help get children and young people a better deal wherever they live?

The majority of young people felt that there should be more activities for them. They think that villages get forgotten because they are small. The younger people thought that ice skating, bowling and discos should be closer. A quarter of the young people interviewed thought that it would be 'brilliant' for young people to run conferences. The same amount thought it would be good to help choose staff for jobs, for example head teachers. The young people also said putting adverts about the charity in magazines and newspapers would help. They generally thought more activities should be localised.

We need some grass in our playground

"Quotes"

There should be things for all ages, and things that we'd all enjoy

Talk to the Government about [us], that's what I would say

We need more facilities, more activities, after-school activities and during school activities, say in lunchtime, and what not. And if we can get together and do all that for ourselves, I think that our community can be a better place

Over there you can see that the goal posts are our dustbins. We need proper goalposts so we can play football

We need grass [in our playground]

I think in that building we are not allowed in when it's playtime. When it's raining and when it's sunny we must have a chance to go in that building just to rest or just to study our homework or anything

If they could supply a room for us where we could go for playtime when it's raining and everything, it would be good

Analysis

There need to be more activities which young people can link into. In a village there is more likely to be a bingo hall than an ice rink. Young people go to drugs and smoking because there is nothing else to do - if there were more activities that would help stop bad things. Young people want to be in charge, and to get their views across by running conferences. If young people speak for themselves they are more likely to get listened to.

Young people were not sure about choosing staff but they were OK about having a view expressed. There should always be a young person around when people are being interviewed. Their views should be considered though we know they cannot alone make the decisions. Young people may not feel up to handling interviews and so would need some guidance/ training before doing it. Given the work is about and involves young people, a good impact on young people at an interview is important.

4. OUR FUTURE VISION

These are the main things we think any good charity should do now or help others do:

- have adults that support young people in different ways and that have faith and believe in them;

- involve young people in different activities and help councils to open youth clubs and sports centres so that young people have more things to do after school;

- when adults make decisions about young people and children they should make sure that they are involved or are there to say their views;

- try to involve everyone around the country;

- have more research done with and by young people as this research we have done was very successful;

- other young people organising like Article 12 which stands up for young people;

- produce a young people's magazine written by young people.

Let young people have a say

5. WHAT ALL ADULTS SHOULD DO

We want every adult who comes into contact with young people to respond positively in schools, homes and in the community to the voices and opinions of the world's young generation.

These are the adults we want to speak out to through our project:

- parents
- people who work in education
- teachers and head teachers
- social workers
- college lecturers
- youth workers
- doctors
- health workers
- councillors
- press/media
- people who work with fostered and adopted young people
- youth treatment officers and people who work in secure units
- politicians
- and all people who work in the community

We hope that parents will support their children but let them have their own lives so they can develop into their own person, a person that children can have an equal relationship with, a relationship that we, as children now, are striving for. We hope that parents will take their children's views and opinions into account when making family decisions so that young people will feel that their feelings and their lives are important, and hopefully relationships between parents and their children will become stronger.

We want teachers to listen to pupils' views on subjects so their choice of subjects will be wider, making young people feel more comfortable at school and more optimistic about their future.

We hope doctors will be more sensitive to the needs and feelings of young people so they will be more confident when approaching their doctor with a problem.

We are looking forward to youth and social workers working in harmony with young people in residential establishments (and at home) so we will feel more comfortable in our home and environment.

We hope people in our community will respect each other so young people will grow up knowing and experiencing respect and positive relationships between everyone in every community.

6. SIGNING OFF

And so we reach the conclusion. Almost a year's hard work is finally gathered here. We have found that young people are concerned about drugs, bullying, racism and relationships. We now know that peer pressure is a worry to hormone stormed teenagers and that most young people believe that adults do not understand them, particularly parents and teachers.

Young people feel that MPs don't understand 'real' people
(God knows what happened to the fake ones).

When asked the question: 'do young people want to have a say?' we were greeted with an ear shattering 'YES!' and when we asked why is it important, the majority of the next generation said that adults should not be the only ones to have a say.

We have learned that some young people would actually be willing to attend meetings and an annual reception (there is hope!).

We'd like to finish with a much loved quote from a young person:

'we are the future, we are part of the world as well, we know what we want but we just need help to get it'